# Branching Out
## Creating a sustainable garden extension

Mona Abboud

This book is dedicated to Jay Cockrell, without whom none of this could have happened.

With grateful thanks to Bryan Hewitt, for his invaluable help; to Steve Caplin, Renaissance man extraordinaire, who, yet again, brought his own special brand of magic; Chris Daynes, my long-suffering solicitor, whose patience, dedication and perseverance got us over the line; Herculean Charlie Harris, who stepped in when necessary and vanquished many heavy tasks; Peter Reader, for his helpful advice, and for lending me his son Ed to help out; and of course Alan Dallman, who was kind enough to sell me part of his precious garden.

All contents © Mona Abboud 2024
Published by Wood Vale Publishing
monasgarden.co.uk
First published March 2024
ISBN no 978-1-7385658-0-1
Edited and designed by Steve Caplin

# Out of my mind?

**A**T THE AGE OF **71** most lifelong gardeners would be resting in their hammocks, if not on their laurels. So why on earth would I choose to embark on the biggest and most challenging task of my horticultural life: buying a neighbouring 600 square metres of overgrown scrubland and adding it to my award-winning garden? Knowing full well the back-breaking physical work this would involve, as well as the huge expense and stress it would inevitably entail? As my friend Steve put it when he first saw the plot: "You must be out of your bloody mind."

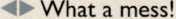 What a mess!

# In the beginning

*I*N 1999 I MOVED to this terraced house in Muswell Hill, north London. What attracted me to this property was the 100 metre garden, a narrow twisting strip which widens at the bottom.

It was a blank canvas, a featureless stretch of grass. It gave me the opportunity to create an oasis filled with unusual plants from all over the world. I chose to focus particularly on New Zealand plants – most particularly on Corokia. Since December 2015 I have been the proud National Collection Holder of this genus.

▶ The new generation of Corokias

▼ The garden in 2020, courtesy of Apple Maps

# The bequest

THE QUESTION REMAINS: why would I want to take on such a big challenge at this stage of my life? The most important factor behind my keenness to purchase this land – verging on an obsession – is that at the end of 2021 I decided to bequest my garden and house to Perennial, The Gardeners' Royal Benevolent Society. This charity would ensure that my garden would survive and carry on into the future.

The new extension would be an added bonus, particularly with the proposed installation of a new large greenhouse which would allow the propagation and dissemination of a new generation of Corokia which have been seeding themselves freely in my garden, as well as other unusual New Zealand plants.

This new generation of Corokias recently received a big boost when my friend Paul Boosey of County Park Nursery

in Hampshire (see my book *Corokia – My Adventure*) discovered sixty baby Corokia seedlings in his gravel area. He decided to give them to me, as he knew that my passion for Corokia meant that I would be able to nurture them. This proved to be a great blessing, particularly as many Corokias have been decimated throughout the UK, including in the RHS gardens at Wisely and Hyde Hall, due to the extreme weather conditions and the brutal December of 2022. A case of 'death and resurrection'. My new site would be able to give some of them a new home.

Having run out out of space in my existing garden, this new acquisition would afford me the opportunity for adding to my planting scheme and trying out a new way to create this new garden.

I decided to take on an additional challenge: to make this new environment sustainable by using all the materials afforded by the site itself: not only the logs and branches from the felled trees and cut back stems of the overgrown shrubs, but also lumps of the concrete base on which the previous dilapidated greenhouse sat. By recycling and reusing all this material, I would dramatically reduce the garden's carbon footprint.

# The challenge

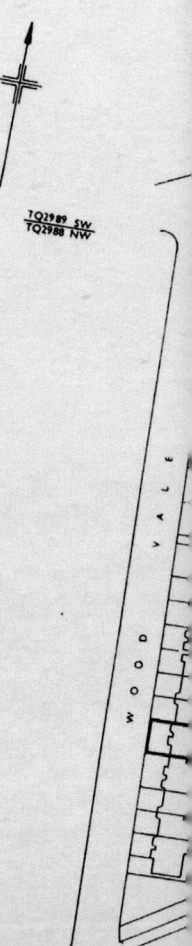

THE WHOLE PROCESS of acquiring the new land proved to be lengthy and tortuous, strewn with setbacks and unforeseen challenges. All along the way it felt like 'two steps forward, one step back'.

I had been encouraged by the previous CEO of Perennial, Peter Newman, to contact my neighbour and owner of this plot, Alan, with an offer. I approached the situation with great misgivings.

Although Alan and I were mostly on friendly terms over the last twenty plus years – both of us keen gardeners, opening our gardens every year for charity – we nevertheless had a few, rather petty, altercations to do with bonfires. Having berated me once, with a few choice words, for lighting a short fire at the end of January at the crack of dawn, he then proceeded to have a lengthy fire in May in the middle of the day. So I had a go at him along the lines of 'one rule for you and another for me'. After which we hardly had any com-

munication, as now in his late eighties he was never to be seen at the end of his garden and so our paths never crossed. I didn't know if he still held a grudge.

I asked to meet him and his lovely wife Anne with great trepidation, and went to their house armed with a nice bottle of wine and a signed copy of my book. I needn't have feared: they both gave me a warm welcome. My main worry was that I wasn't at all sure Alan would want to part with even a fraction of his precious garden, even though he hadn't been able to work in it for many years.

So I played my 'Perennial' card, saying that selling me the plot would ensure its survival, and that it would be taken care of after all of us had relinquished 'this mortal coil'. Otherwise we could be faced with yuppies erecting saunas or other undesirable constructions. To my amazement he agreed in principle, pending a valuation of that plot.

A valuer/surveyor was duly appointed. But now my next worry was that the acquisition and afterwards the clearing and development of the site, which had been neglected for over a decade, would prove to be unaffordable. The other potential difficulty was that Alan had borrowed some money from an Equity Release

11

company, and they had to give the go-ahead before the sale could take place. So I waited for the surveyor to come and give his verdict in a state of great anxiety. He proved to be a dapper gentleman of the old school in his early seventies, from a reputable local firm.

I accompanied him on his visit and appraisal of the site – it had been about ten years since I had seen it during one of Alan's garden open days. The end of his plot wasn't visible from my own garden due to bushes and trees blocking the view, and seeing it again after all this time was a shock. The whole area was flooded – probably courtesy of the Moselle, a river that flows through Tottenham towards the Lea Valley – which also tends to flood my own garden after heavy rain.

The main greenhouse was totally dilapidated. It had sunk with time, and was surrounded by broken glass. An eclectic mix of abandoned objects was strewn everywhere: broken tools, a large gas canister, an old radio, lots of earthenware pots, half of them broken.

A large enclosure surrounded by netting and supported by metal rods for the protection of raspberry plants, was taking a large amount of space, and one could see the spent stems within. The rest of the plot had been totally invaded by brambles and ivy, and the shrubs planted there – mostly

▶ The clearing starts

▶ The netting enclosure for Alan's raspberry plants

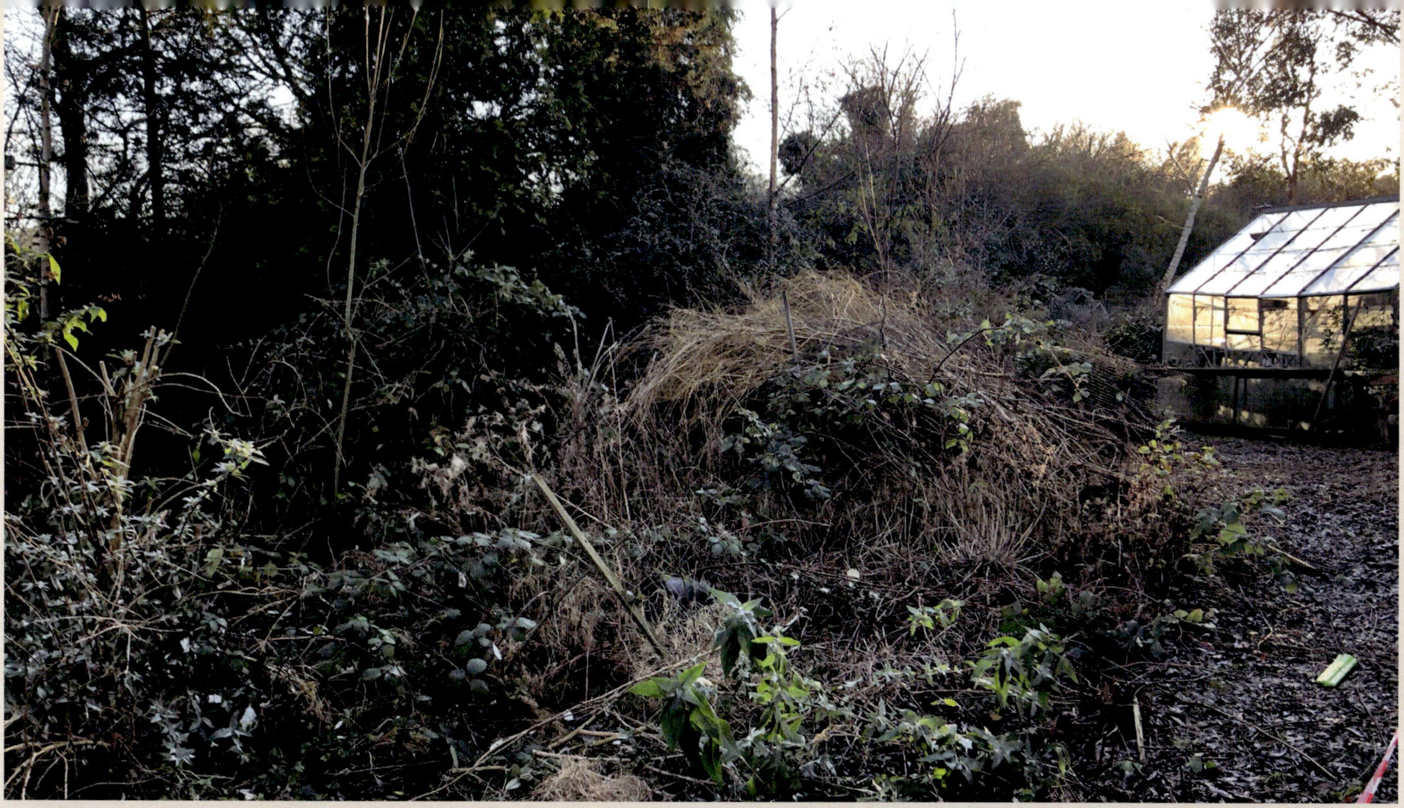

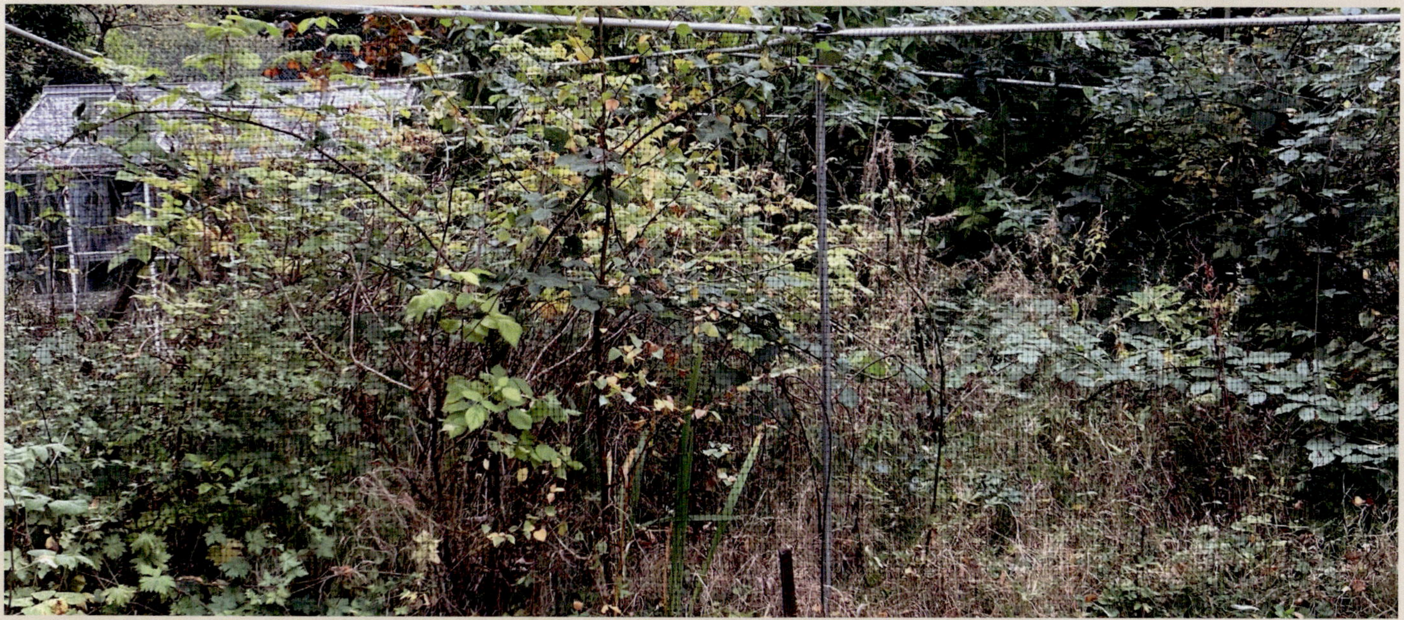

Portuguese laurels, cotoneaster, pyracantha and euonymus – were wildly overgrown. One look at the surveyors's expression made it clear that he wasn't impressed. I'm sure he was wondering why anybody in their right mind would want to buy this junkyard.

But my neighbour had also planted many now beautiful mature trees, including several silver birches and maples, as well as a large oak and a magnolia. These are already giving my new garden a readymade structure.

There were unexpected surprises as well: a few ferns enjoying their semi-shade positions near the trees, a ginkgo biloba and a fig tree which had been cut right back but was sprouting from the base. The gingko only appeared once the growing season was well under way, as it was hidden amongst a pile of large round logs near the entrance to the site – the remnants of a huge eucalyptus which had been felled over fifteen years ago after it became unsafe.

After a nailbiting weekend the surveyor submitted his report and called me to say that the plot had no intrinsic commercial value, citing its lack of access except via a narrow alleyway, and its present state. It couldn't be used for anything, except perhaps as an allotment. Therefore it would only fetch a modest sum.

▲ A laurel which needed to be hacked back

◄ The ginkgo biloba, hidden among the logs

► One of the maples left behind by Alan

15

Old garden meets new extension

# The legal tangle

I WENT BACK TO THE NEIGHBOURS with a reasonable offer which was considerably higher than the one proposed by the surveyor, in order to seal the deal. The offer was accepted. It was a great relief to have overcome the first hurdle. Now the legal process could begin.

A solicitor was instructed to act for Alan, and my own long-standing solicitor Chris took charge of things on my behalf. The Equity Release company was duly notified and immediately demanded some money to conduct their own survey and come up with a valuation.

But Alan's solicitor dragged his heels. He didn't reply to my solicitor's letters and emails, and treated his own elderly client with a marked lack of respect – refusing to take his calls and failing to respond to messages. We were all at our wits' end, and my frustration knew no bounds. Alan must have sensed this, so in January 2022 he gave me the green light to start work on the garden extension, despite the fact that we didn't yet have a contract.

▶ The original entrance point into the new site

# A thorny problem

THE FIRST MAMMOTH TASK was to deal with one of my own self-inflicted problems. Years ago I had planted Kiftsgate, one of the most vigorous and invasive of rambling roses. It was intended to block the unsightly view of Alan's garden. It ended up climbing all over the self-seeded damson trees on his side of the fence, as well as taking over part of the alleyway. Not the sort of 'branching out' I had in mind!

When it flowered in June it looked stunning – an explosion of lovely white blooms. But as all gardeners know, this rose is a rampant thug and its stems reach 10 cm in diameter and 10 metres in length. Dismantling that monster was no mean feat.

Luckily I had the help of one of my gardening heroes, Jay Cockrell. Normally he worked for a London-based garden company creating outdoor spaces for clients all over the capital. At the time he was taking time off from them, and was therefore able to give me a few days a week in order to break the back of this big project.

◀ The white blooms of Kiftsgate, a thug of a rambling rose

Thanks to a four-metre-long ladder and his six foot four height, he was able to reach the stems to be cut back.

While he was doing that I was busy chopping them into manageable disposable sizes. The rose fought back tooth and thorn! Amid what looked like a war zone, Jay and I battled it out for over a week, and finally the monster was vanquished. But in order to prevent it sprouting from the base like a Hydra the whole enormous root needed to be dug up.

Enter Bryan. He had worked at Myddelton Gardens – the brainchild of botanist Edward Bowles – for over thirty years in a senior capacity before taking early retirement. Bryan kindly accepted to come and help me in the garden – he has been coming here twice a month for the last three years and has proved indispensable in keeping my existing garden up to scratch, whilst also giving a hand in the development of the new site.

To him was given the unenviable task of excavating what remained of the Kiftsgate thug. Bryan is nothing if not persistent, but it took a while. In the end he managed to get the whole root out.

▶ The four-metre ladder needed to reach Kiftsgate's high branches

◀▼ My heroes Jay (left) and Bryan (below)

# Permission granted

**D**ISASTER NEARLY STRUCK from another quarter. Alan suddenly announced that he was moving, and therefore selling his house and garden. I panicked, fearing that now he would have no incentive to sell me part of his garden and wouldn't want the bother of dealing with our transaction and the headache it had become.

On top of that the Equity Release people who came to do the survey insisted on visiting the house as well as the

garden in order to put a value on both. Alan understandably deemed it unnecessary and intrusive and threw them out.

Thankfully a week later, as February dragged on, things took a calmer turn, and Alan allowed the survey of his house to take place, whilst Chris drew up a contract committing my neighbours to sell me the piece of land at the agreed price. The contract was then signed by all parties and the Equity Release company gave oral permission for the sale to go ahead.

▼ The garden after the purchase of the new land, indicated in green

◀▲ Time to get on with the clearing

27

Hands-on clearing

# The war zone

**B**ACK IN THE WAR ZONE, the felling of dead trees and the pruning of overgrown shrubs — *euonymus, cotoneaster* and Portuguese laurel — got underway. Jay even managed to fell one of the ugly conifers single handedly.

March heralded the start of spring, and brought with it torrential rain which flooded most of the site. We had to use planks to move between the different areas.

◀ Jay fells an ugly conifer

▶ Pruning at its most extreme

▶ Planks are needed to get around the flooded site

Having cleared a substantial amount of brambles and ivy, a bonfire quickly disposed of the lot, including the remnants of the monstrous Kiftsgate. But there was an upside: the burning produced a welcome quantity of ash, which would be used to enrich the soil.

Setting the ivy and brambles alight

▲ Dismantling the old greenhouse

# March to April

Towards the end of March the weather warmed up considerably and the temperature even reached 18°C. This was perfect timing for the gardening contractors I had booked to dismantle the dilapidated greenhouses and to take them away, along with other unwanted leftovers.

In order to deal with the constant flooding the men brought in a digger to gouge the earth throughout the site,

▲ Digging trenches to install drainage pipes

▲ The pipe leads to a drainage sump

so that drainage pipes could be installed leading to a sump at the very bottom of the garden. Some of the fencing was removed in order to fit in a new gate and access the site. The concrete base on which the old greenhouse stood was partially broken down and taken away as well – all this during the course of just one week!

As April hove into view, the completion papers were finally signed by all parties to everyone's immense relief, six long months after the whole process had begun. My poor valiant solicitor Chris must have felt it as keenly as well, and I'm sure he was delighted to see the end of this whole frustrating business. But for me this was very much still the beginning.

# Carbon neutral

**I**REALISED EARLY ON that in order to achieve my sustainable carbon neutral mission I needed to do a huge amount of recycling, for which some serious power tools would be required. So I purchased a battery-powered chainsaw and a Makita drill, as well as a huge shredder aptly named 'Titan'. This would allow the shredding of branches to produce wood chips, and the cutting up of branches and tree trunks into logs which would delineate the paths and borders.

I also received help from a different quarter: my long-standing and trusted tree surgeon Julian and his team, who had been dealing with my trees for over fifteen years, came to give me a hand by felling three more ugly conifers. Jay then sawed the trunks into the requisite log sizes and shredded the branches. Meanwhile we also resumed the clearing of the persistent ivy and self-seeded sycamore saplings, and by May I was finally able to start planting (*see appendix – new plants*).

▶ The mighty Titan in action

37

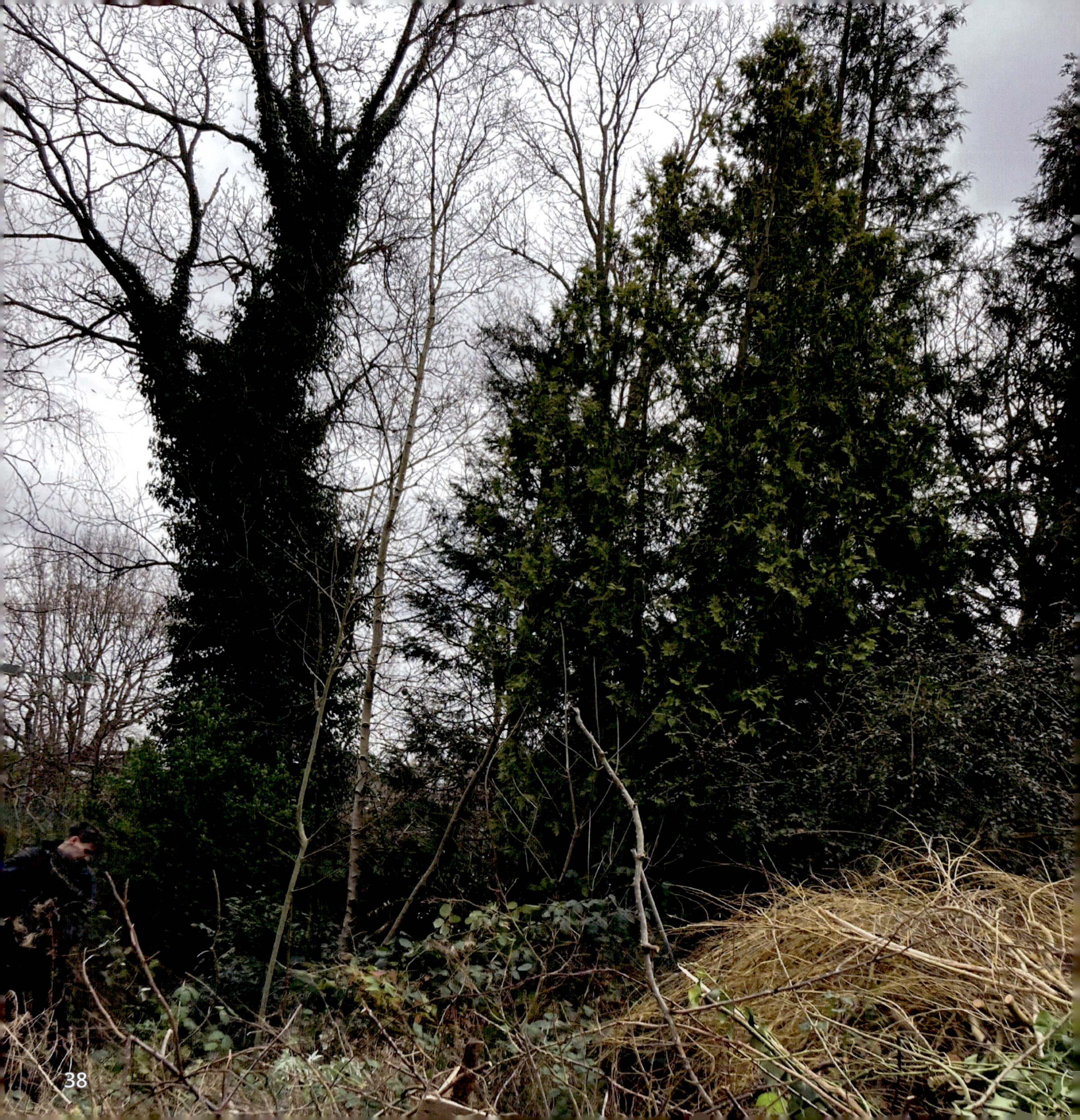

◀ Three ugly conifers felled…   ▲ …and repurposed

39

We still had to deal with the concrete, which had only been partially removed, at the location of the old greenhouse. The Makita drill came into play, and lumps of concrete and hardcore were painstakingly removed.

By this time the drought conditions which had started in June, following on the heels of a very dry spring, reached apocalyptic proportions with a temperature of 39.9°C on July 19th. So endless daily watering sessions were added to all the other tasks. I spent three hours every day at the end of a hose from June to mid August, when the weather finally relented and it started raining again.

Despite the amount of home-produced mulch-wood chips, 15 tons of topsoil had to be brought in order to create the right conditions for exotic plants. The remaining concrete and hardcore underneath would hopefully help with the drainage.

▲ The future exotic area – hard to believe

▶ The topsoil brought in, and evened out

41

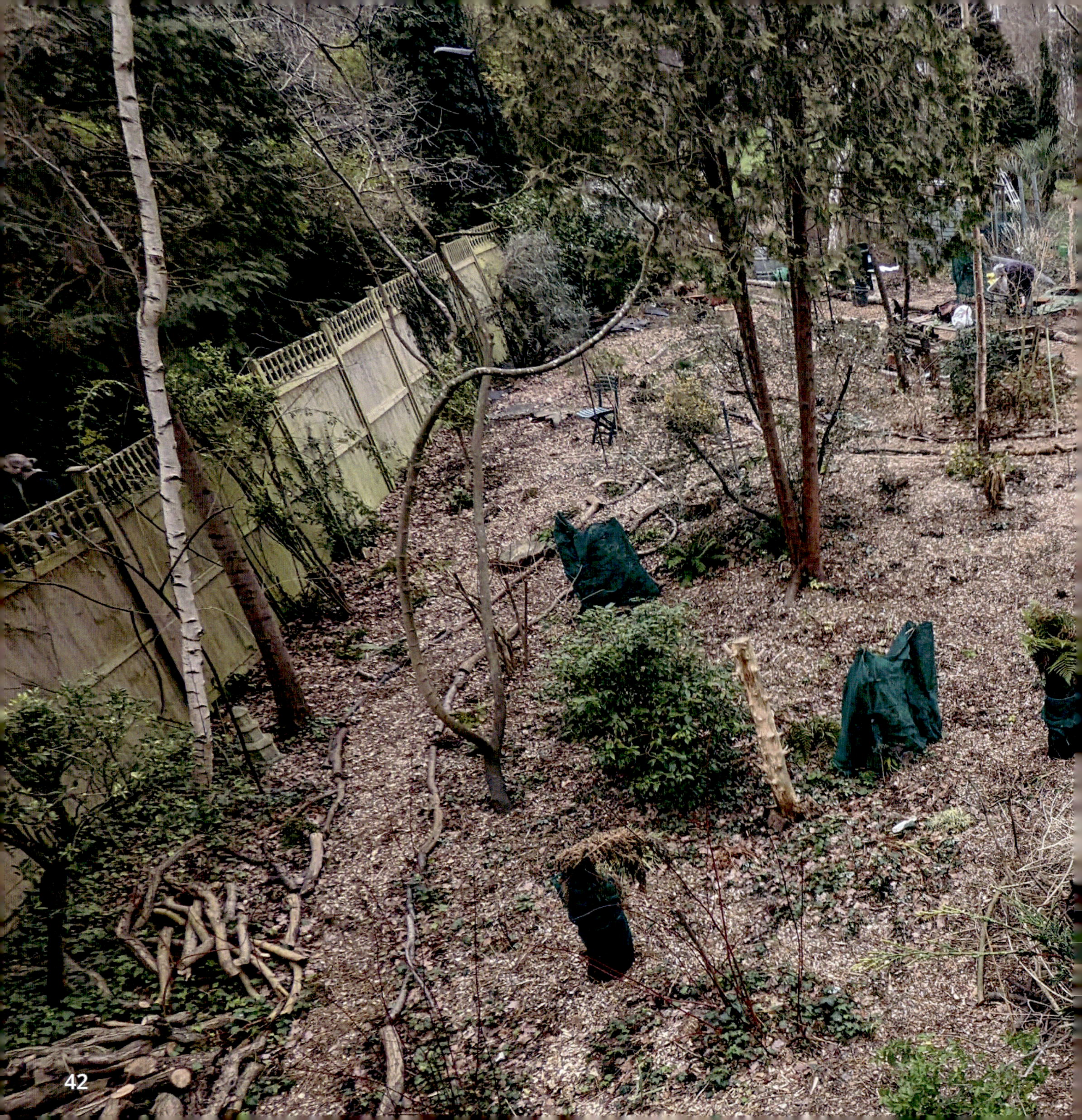

Preparing the ground

# Planting starts

*I*SPENT SOME TIME choosing plants for the exotic and Mediterranean areas, which were provided by the Palm Centre in Richmond. These were duly delivered at the beginning of September. This should have been a relatively straightforward operation despite the 100 plus yards of alleyway to negotiate, were it not for the huge olive tree weighing 200 kilos and over seven feet tall including the large pot. Alarm bells – literally – started ringing the day before delivery, as I received several calls from the Palm Centre. They wanted to make sure there would be someone strong on hand to help with the transportation of the tree. Jay promised to be there.

◀ Leftover sawn eucalyptus logs – a creative way to frame the exotic plants

▶ Manhandling the olive tree into the garden, with help from two German cameramen

On the next day as the moment arrived and the big lorry carrying all the plants appeared and parked on the main road, the olive tree looked even more enormous than when I had seen it at the Palm Centre. An older man came out of the lorry – he later told us he was 62, and had recently undergone a knee operation – and my heart sank.

Somehow he and Jay managed to lower the olive onto a trolley and wheel it down the alleyway. The difficulty arose once they reached the gate entrance. Trolley plus tree were much higher than the top of the gate, so needed to come in at an angle.

As providence would have it, a lady from a German TV company and two cameramen had arrived at the same time to visit the garden, and the two cameramen were persuaded to help out. So Jay and the driver, plus the two Germans, pushed and panted and swore – a few heartfelt *'verdammt noch mal!'* loosely translated as 'bloody hell' could be heard – and finally coaxed the trolley up the slight ramp. It was wet due to a recent downpour, and caused the earth to sink under the heavy weight.

Despite all that not only did they get it into the site, but also managed to offload the tree very near its final planting position. The other plants, including two tall cypresses, were brought in without any problem.

◀ The newly installed *Dicksonia antarctica*

As if all this drama wasn't enough excitement for a week, a couple of days later I braved the outer reaches of High Barnet, driving down a long dirt track between two suburban houses to reach a specialist tree fern nursery. There I bought a nearly two metre *Dicksonia antarctica* tree fern, which was then manhandled into my car in front of the passenger seat and fastened like a VIP.

At the other end I dragged it out, hoicked it up my front steps, through the house and down the steps from the conservatory onto the patio. I stupidly decided not to wheel it down the alleyway because I felt it would take too long, instead strapping it to my trolley with near flat

▲ The second burning of ivy and brambles produced a lot of useful ash

tyres and pushing it down my 300 foot long garden and into the extension, and finally down the new path and into a good place in the woodland area. Definitely my exercise for the day! Getting it out of its pot and planting it was the easy part. Worth the effort though, as it's now looking magnificent in its semi-shaded spot.

As the weather settled into autumn, the second ceremonial burning took place. All the ivy, brambles and *pyracantha* branches went up in flames. It was all over very quickly as the pile was bone dry and didn't create much smoke at all. On top of the ash I subsequently added all the organic matter at my disposal.

# Planting the olive

**N**EXT CAME THE PLANTING of the large olive tree. It took all three of us and several days to dig the huge hole, dispose of the clay, add topsoil, compost and gravel to improve the drainage, and finally ease the tree into its final position.

Planting the tree was a mammoth task for the poor chaps, having to manhandle this giant of a tree out of its pot and into its pre-prepared hole.

▲ Planting the olive tree

▶ The tree in its final position

48

49

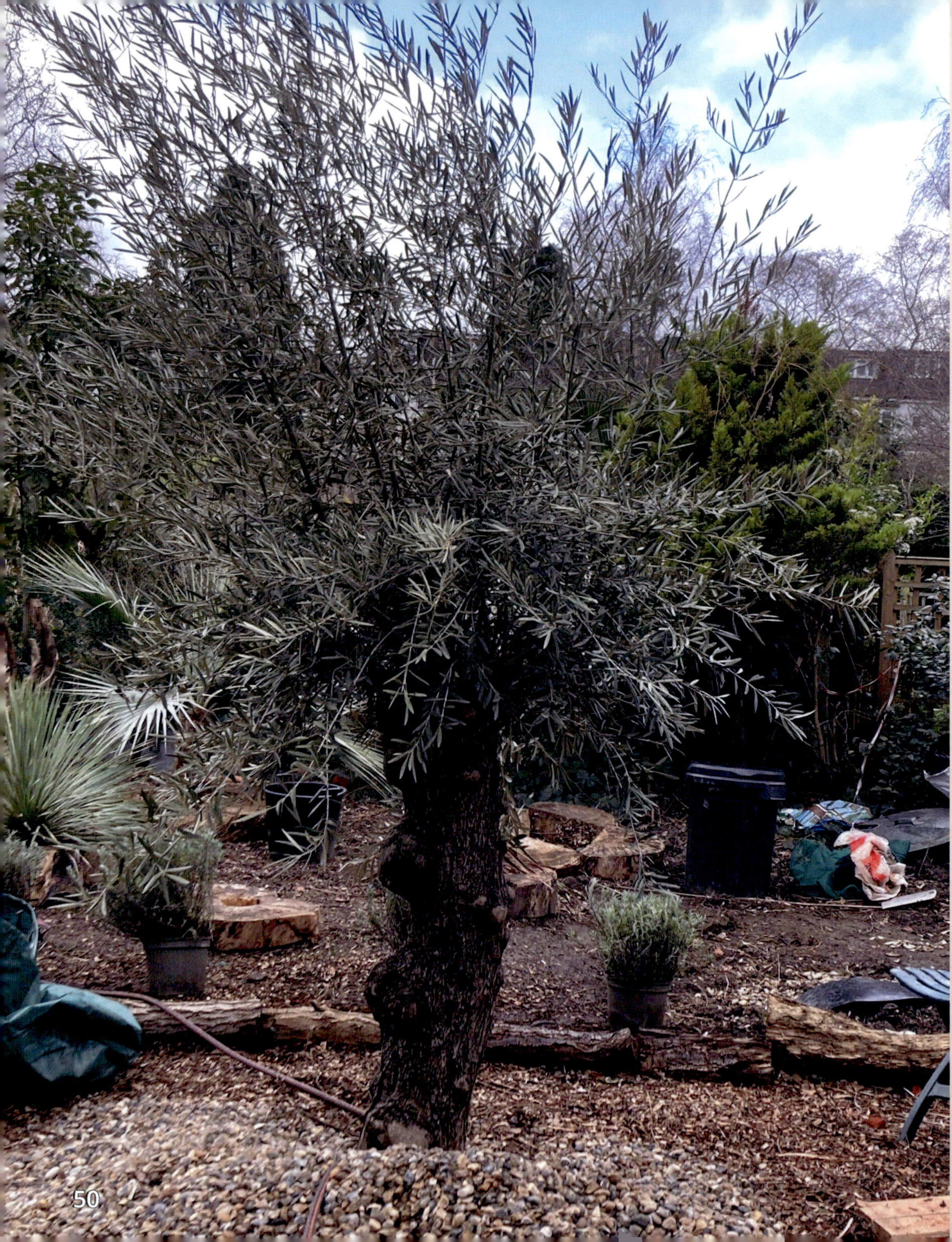

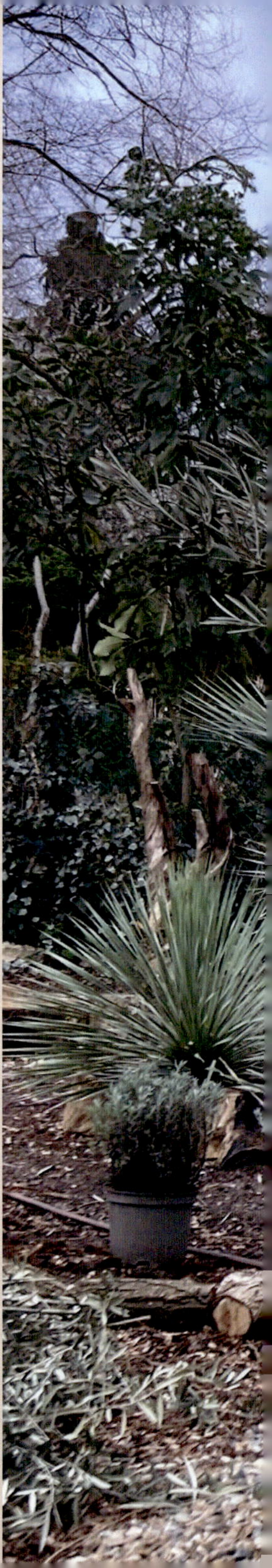

The olive tree
before and after
pruning

51

# Floods and chips

After the incredibly dry summer we had just lived through, autumn proved to be mild and generally very wet. By November both my gardens were flooded, as was the newly planted olive tree. So Jay and I had to dig a trench and install another drainage pipe to evacuate the water away from the olive tree, as the new sump at the bottom of the garden had clearly not managed to absorb it all.

We carried on with the hard landscaping, creating another path cutting through the woodland area and rejoining the main one. We couldn't complete the task as we were short of logs to trace the new contours. Yet again luck was on

◀ Covering the drainage pipe with broken pots

▲ Pollarding the weeping willow created a vast pile of wood chips

our side, and we would soon acquire more timber than we could possibly hope for. Julian, my faithful tree surgeon, came back with his team to pollard the giant weeping willow in next door's garden. This venerable tree has been a landmark for all neighbouring gardens but now, at over seventy years old, it has become seriously compromised as the the main part of its trunk was hollow. The neighbour whose tree it was decided that it needed cutting back severely in order to stop it crashing down in high wind. This proved to be a bonus for all concerned, as Julian could leave me with the logs and branches in order to fulfil my needs, thereby saving him time and effort – as there would be no clearing away necessary – and the neighbour money.

On top of that Julian was able to shred most of the branches using my very own Titan, whilst his team carried on sawing off the willow limbs. I ended up with a mountain of wood chips. Julian's parting words were: 'This won't be enough, I promise you'. I thought he was exaggerating, but time proved him right.

▲ A covering of snow

# Winter strikes

A FEW DAYS AFTER JULIAN'S VISIT winter hit us suddenly. The temperature dropped like a stone, accompanied by six inches of snow, which lasted over a week in the freezing conditions. I had to go round the garden with a broom trying to shake off the snow from all the evergreen shrubs and tender plants.

▲ Conifer logs from the felled trees make an effective border

▲ Two cypresses form the entrance to next door's garden

Once the thaw returned, and as the year was drawing to a close, Bryan and I were able create a narrow raised strip flanked by conifer logs on the boundary with the neighbours in order to plant Mediterranean type shrubs and trees (*see appendix*). We placed two tall cypresses marking the entrance to next door's garden, standing proudly like two sentinels.

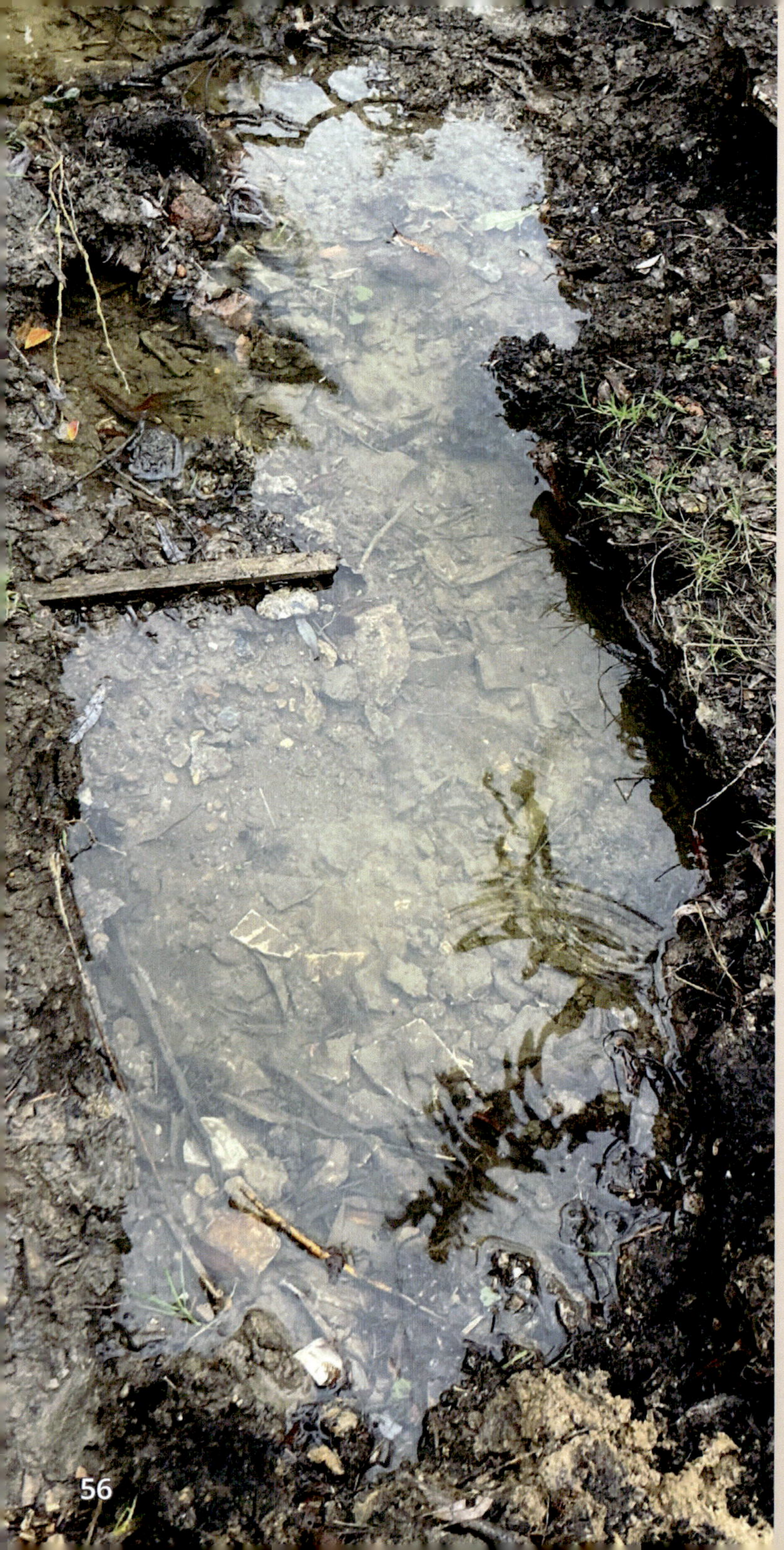

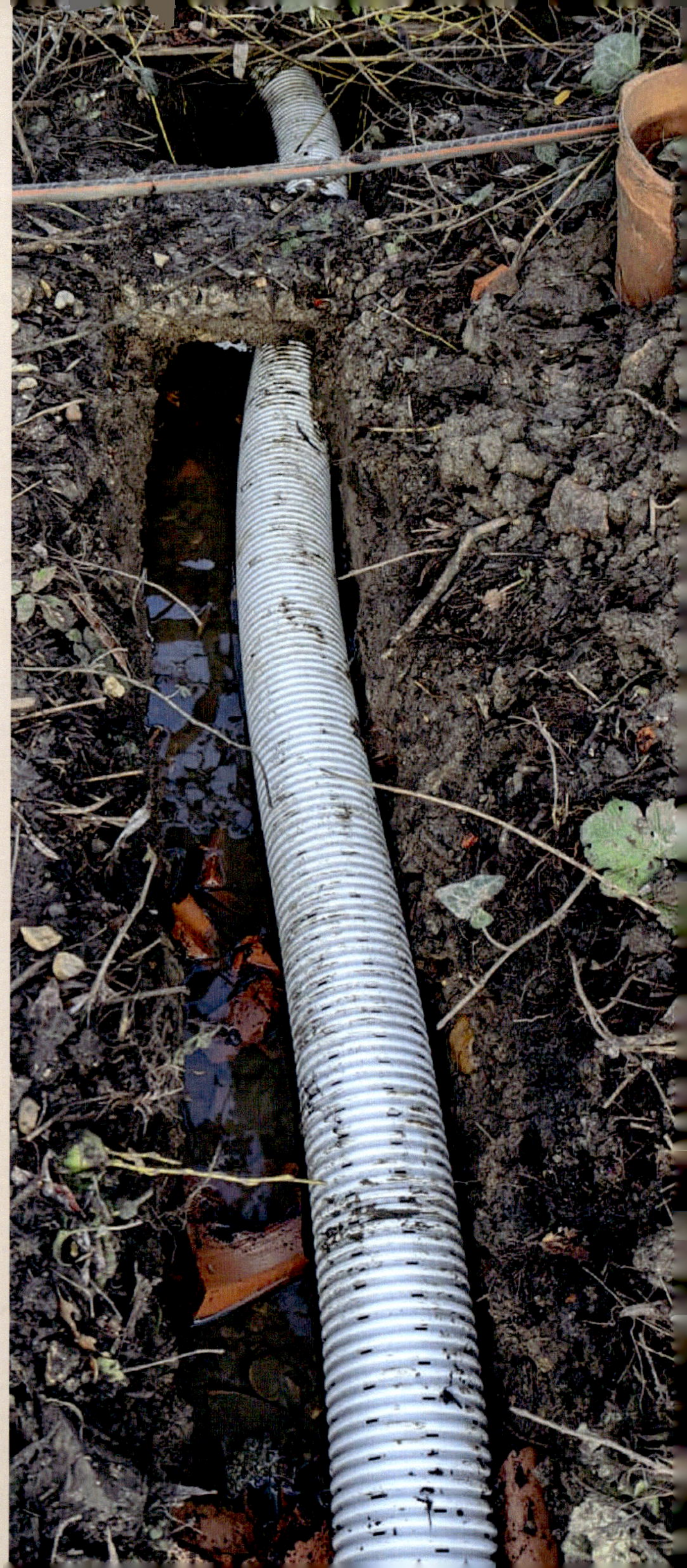

# New year floods

**O**N THE MORNING of the first of January 2023, while most people were still nursing their hangovers, I was out in the garden starting out as I meant to go on with my five a day: not fruit and vegetables, but barrows full of wood chips to be spread around the whole garden. I had inherited the typical London clay, which had turned to concrete during the previous baking summer and produced large cracks everywhere.

Now, in January, the earth had turned into slippery glue. In order to get through that mountain of wood chips, 105 barrows – I counted them – would be filled and emptied in the course of the next few months.

During that time, due to the recent flooding, a lot of excess water was still trapped under the concrete, which we hadn't managed to dig up – the remnants of the foundations for the old greenhouse. Some of that water had seeped from under it to inundate the large olive tree below. So more drilling and excavating, and more installation of drain pipes.

◀ Drainage pipes control the flooding

# The greenhouse

*I*WAS TRYING TO FIND A BRICKLAYER willing to build the low wall for my proposed new greenhouse. This was proving nigh impossible. One would have thought I was wanting to build one of the big greenhouses at Kew! Though reasonably large at six metres long by three wide, the wall was only going to be 70 cm high.

Some builders came up with some ridiculously high quotes. In the end I went with a small outfit recommended by Bryan which I hesitated to employ at first as I wasn't sure about the boss, a gentleman of the old school.

But as time was pressing and the fitters recommended by the company providing the greenhouse itself hadn't come back to me, I resigned myself to letting him start in early February. The challenge was the lack of direct access except via the alleyway. For three days, first a digger then another small vehicle carrying bricks, sand and mortar trundled up and down that passageway, narrowly missing all the locals walking their dogs and women with children in pushchairs.

As the digging for the foundations of the greenhouse began, I faced the problem of where to deposit the two feet of soil, mostly clay, that was being excavated. The only possible place was the proposed prairie/herbaceous border area, the one I had so lovingly prepared with layer upon layer of choice organic matter. But there was nothing for it, and all that lovely soil was soon covered with the excess clay and flattened with the digger. Back to square one, and an environment now far from ideal for cultivating grasses and other plants all requiring very free-draining soil.

▲ The foundations for the greenhouse

▲ Building the greenhouse

The greenhouse wall was finally satisfactorily completed by the end of February, despite a few delays and lame excuses for absence.

Finding a fitter to erect the rest of the building took longer. I went cap in hand to the greenhouse company and begged them to find me someone for the job.

By this time I was worried that it wouldn't be finalised in time for a group of Austrians who were due to visit the garden in May. Luckily they persuaded their best fitter to send a brilliant 22 year old, who put up the rest of the building in a day before Easter. Inside we installed the staging left behind by Alan on which to stand the tender plants.

The greenhouse now stands proudly at the end of the new plot, a focal point with all the paths leading to it. This coincided with the coming together of the hard landscaping, with all the paths outlined with conifer and willow logs. We used the builders' sand and the bricks left behind by the bricklayers as hardcore.

Lavenders frame different areas

Bricks and sand left by the builders act as hardcore

# The coir solution

*I*SPENT MANY ANXIOUS HOURS racking my brain in order to come up with a quick solution to the problem of how to mitigate the excess clay. I didn't want to delay the start of the planting, but also couldn't afford the time and effort to import tons of sand, topsoil and grit and wheel it down all the way from the top of the road to the new garden. This would also upset my carbon neutral aims.

As time went on I grew more and more frustrated. I had heard about the Swedish plantsman Peter Korn, who was pioneering the method of growing everything in sand, including trees. But this wasn't a practical solution for me.

Then suddenly one very early morning I woke up with a stroke of inspiration.

There was a medium I had been using successfully for the last few years for improving the drainage of the soil, but also for cosmetic purposes in order to give the earth a reddish Mediterranean/exotic look: coir.

▲ A block of coir

Coir is a versatile natural fibre extracted from the husk of the coconut fruit. It is highly sustainable in comparison to peat moss. Though it isn't completely carbon neutral, its great advantage is that its super light, and its dry form reduces shipping costs while being environmentally conscious – 178 kg $CO_2$ per ton once hydrated – which gets further reduced by the fact that a single ton of coir can create 14 tons of product, making coir's eco credentials clear as day (see www.carbongold.com). Eventually all the plants in the prairie area were sunk in a cocoon of coir and have since thrived as a result.

# Prairie planting

Now the planting up of the prairie area could begin in earnest. However before I could use the blocks of coir for that purpose I hit a snag with one of the batches I had purchased previously from a nursery in Suffolk during one of my occasional visits there. They didn't respond to the adding of water, unlike the ones I'd used before, and refused to expand and break down into the usual crumbly consistency.

Thankfully help was at hand in the form of Charlie, Jay's friend and flatmate, a giant of a man whom I nicknamed 'Hercules'. Within a few hours he managed to beat the whole lot into submission by bashing them expertly and drowning them in water butts. So now, with Bryan's help, I was able to move a large number of my herbaceous plants and grasses from my existing garden and relocate them in the prairie area (*see appendix*).

I dug up at least fifty *Libertia peregrinans*, and placed them in the continuation of the new row of lavender, where they framed the two *olearia capillaris* and *paniculata*, as well as Corokia seedlings, which are an important addition to my already extensive collection of New Zealand shrubs. I repositioned other plants throughout the rest of the garden as well — all part of the recycling (*see appendix*).

The seedlings had appeared in my garden under the Corokia hedge a couple of years previously, and are now awaiting adulthood in their permanent abode. They are yet to be named.

▲ Charlie bashing the coir into submission

◀ *Olearia paniculata*

The prairie ready to go

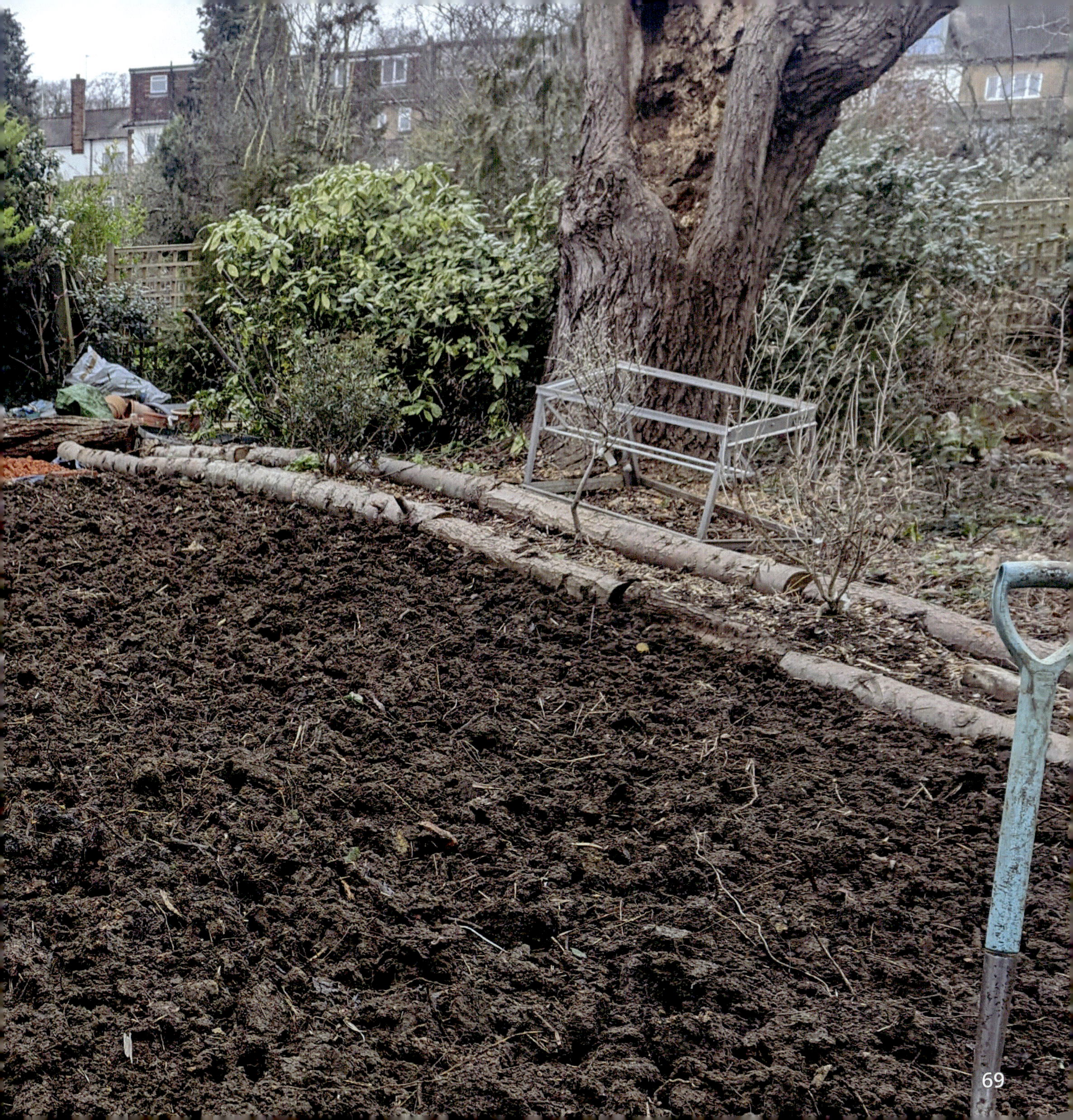

# Bench repair

APART FROM THE GREENHOUSE STAGING, eucalyptus logs and a huge quantity of earthenware pots, my neighbour Alan bequeathed me some garden furniture as well: a very fine set of 1930s oak chairs, together with a table and long seat plus a cast iron bench. All were in a sorry state and required urgent restoration.

Luckily my brilliant friend Steve Caplin, a true Renaissance man, who along with his many other accomplishments happens to be the creator of quirky and very original furniture in his spare time, made oak replicas of the missing pegs for the 1930s chairs and the long seat, and replaced all the rotten slats of the cast iron bench with new hardwood ones.

Admittedly I could have easily bought a cheap brand new bench on eBay or at B&Q, but this was all part of my recycling project. Steve had them ready for the first visit of the year and the unveiling of the new garden extension.

▲ Steve and Mona on the repaired seats  ▼ The bench with new slats  ▼ The new oak pegs hold the seats together

71

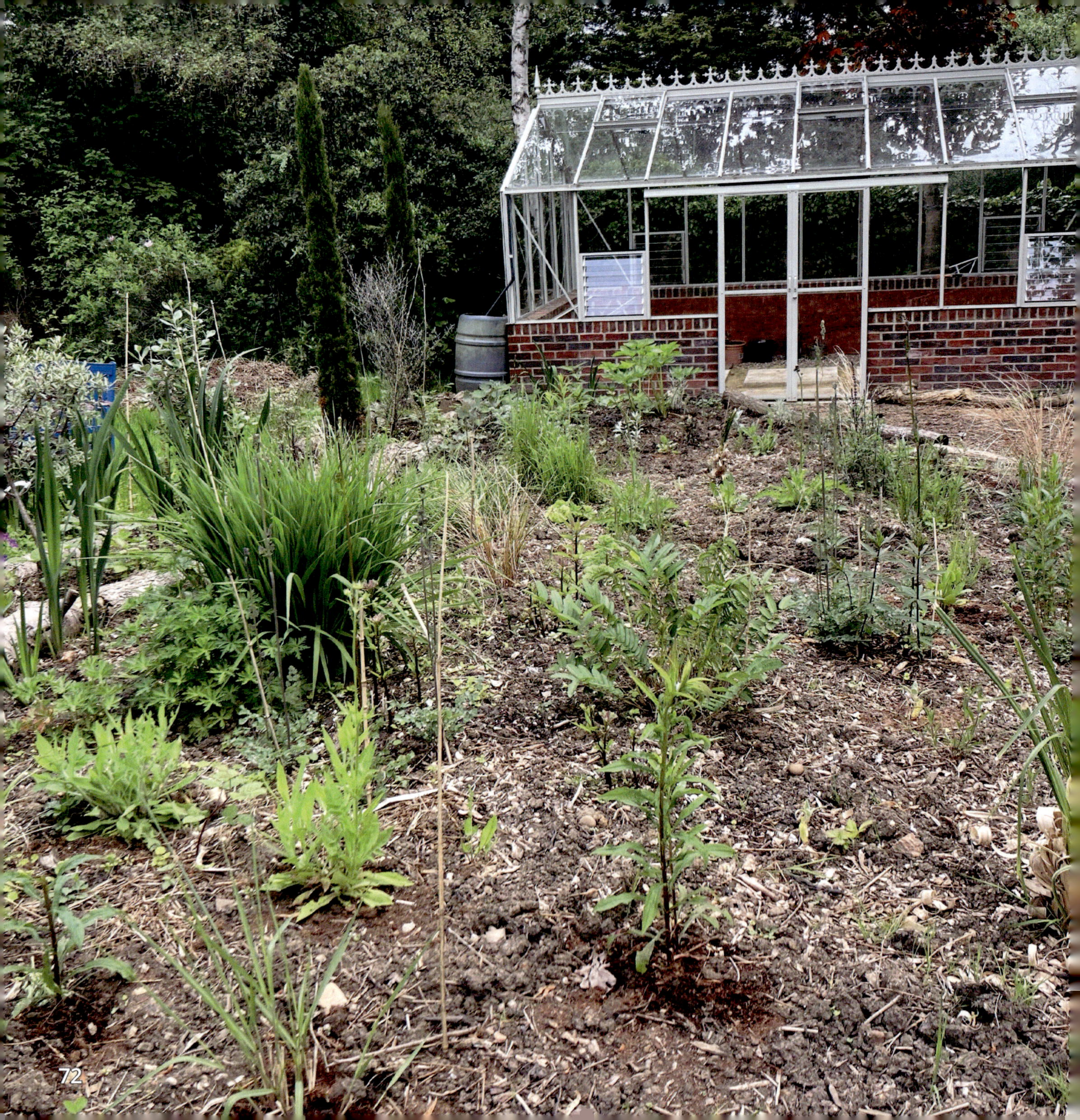

# Chelsea plants

THE AUSTRIANS' VISIT coincided with the Chelsea Flower Show, which attracts many foreign visitors every year, who then spend the week also looking round a few English gardens. They seemed very interested in my new ecologically friendly project, and were intrigued by my unusual plants.

The Chelsea Show gave rise to another event, this one quite unexpected, which felt at first like a mixed blessing. As I've already said, Jay works for a garden company which creates outdoor spaces for clients all over London. This year they had built a Mediterranean show garden at Chelsea, at the end of which all the plants had to be given away.

Jay had mentioned my love for those types of plants and the fact that I cultivated them, and so they kindly offered to give me a few. I submitted a wish list of ten available small ones. But a few days after the Royal Hospital had shut its gates for another year I received a call from Jay

◀ The prairie before the arrival of the Chelsea plants

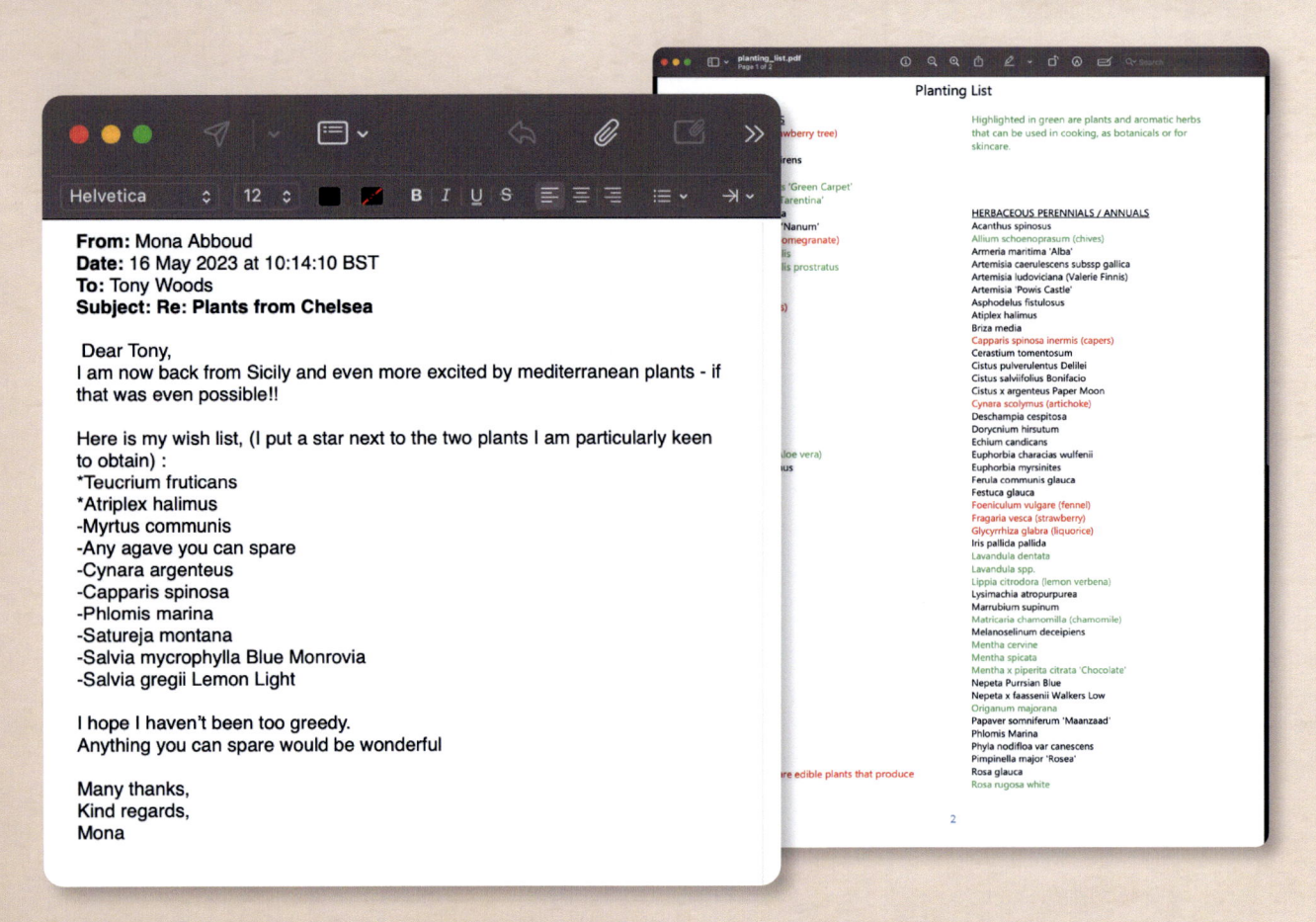

▲ The list of available ex-display plants, and my wish list

saying that their exhibit was being dismantled and that a van was on its way to bring me my plants, and that he and his workmate were following behind in another van. I did find it strange that they would need two vans to deliver my ten small plants, but thought that perhaps I was only the first stop en route to other deliveries.

As the first van fetched up in front of my house, two men got out and started literally chucking one plant after another on my small driveway, a lot of them looking practically dead and quite a few half broken.

My jaw nearly hit the ground. When I'd somewhat recovered from the shock, I protested: 'But I have only asked for ten small plants, and there's about forty here. What do you want me to do with all these half dead things?' One chap retorted 'Not our problem lady. If you don't want them you can give them away. We are just doing what we've been told'. On that abrupt note they drove off.

A while later, while I stood there pondering the situation, Jay and his mate arrived in the second van, this time carrying very large plants in big pots, including several Agaves and one stonking Corokia, with stems growing in all opposite directions – definitely having a 'bad hair' day! How it would have contributed aesthetically to the show garden I couldn't imagine. Nevertheless I appreciated the fact that the boss of the company had felt it was right to give it to me, as the National Collection Holder of this genus.

However nice it was to be given sixty Mediterranean type plants for free, the question now was what to do with them in the immediate future and in that parlous state – particularly as I only had ten days before the next important garden opening, the London Squares and Gardens weekend. It was only the second time I had agreed to participate in that event, and I really wanted to give a good impression, particularly of the new extension.

So, first things first: I begged Jay and his co-worker to give me a hand carrying all the plants down the alleyway and into the new site. They very kindly obliged. It took both of them five journeys to get them all in. Meanwhile I dragged out the hose and embarked on an immediate resuscitation mission by proceeding to drown them all for over an hour. They hadn't been watered for four days of circa 30°C and had totally dried out. Thankfully they all seemed to revive, and I repeated the process over the next few days.

The fifteen salvias that were part of the consignment were half broken through the rough manhandling they had suffered. They were in full flower, having been forced to bloom in time for the show a month earlier than normal. So later on I cut them right back, sacrificing the flowers in order to strengthen them into a healthy regrowth.

After the intensive watering I looked at these unhappy specimens and wondered how it would be possible to have them all in the ground in less than ten days. I must have looked at Jay with something approaching despair. 'Don't worry,' he said, 'we'll manage'.

Once again our herculean Charlie, who happened to be between jobs, came to our aid. A few days later he and Jay attacked the problem with spades and muscle power, as

◀ The shapeless Corokia

the eight large plants needed to end up in eight large holes. We all set to in sweltering heat, trying to lose the clay that we dug up and planting everything in coir and leftover topsoil. The boys grappled with the eight biggies while I dealt with the smaller plants. Over two days of backbreaking work we got everything in, including the salvias. Nothing short of miraculous!

The Corokia was subjected to a drastic haircut but it still looked rather shapeless. At the end of this marathon I was fast asleep by 8pm. After a last minute tidying and watering the garden opened its doors to 163 visitors who, apart from the Austrians, saw the new extension for the very first time. I think it went well.

Some of the Chelsea plants before planting

All the Chelsea plants in place in the prairie

# A sedate summer

After the drama of the Chelsea plants things calmed down, and the rest of the summer proceeded at a much more sedate tempo. More people saw the garden at the NGS opening at the beginning of July, and a group visit of members of the U3A Bromley in August rounded up the summer season.

As it rained regularly during July and August I didn't spend every day at the end of a hose, as I had done the previous summer. Before it drew to a close, that summer had another unexpected gift up its sleeve. By this stage there was no doubt that Julian's prophecy had come to pass, and that the whole mountain of wood chips he had left behind had mostly been gobbled up and digested by the earth and now much more was needed to completely break down the stubborn clay.

My trusty Titan shredder can only produce a small amount of new organic matter as the shreddable material from my garden is limited. How to obtain more without having to buy it in was the conundrum. If I could persuade Julian or another tree surgeon to dump some chippings by the roadside near the entrance to the alleyway it still would require a lot of transporting by wheelbarrow and legally would need to be removed by the end of the day.

The patron saint of gardeners had obviously been aware of my situation, as one early August day as Bryan and I were tackling persistent weeds, he heard the sound of a shredder and chainsaw at full throttle nearby. We went to investigate and found that the noise was coming from the grounds of Georgians Tennis Club on the other side of the alleyway from my garden, where pruning and cutting down of trees was in full swing. There was already a mountain of shredded material lying there. So after talking to the workmen I contacted the manager, who was more than happy to let me take it all away.

▲ Shredded material, courtesy of the tennis club

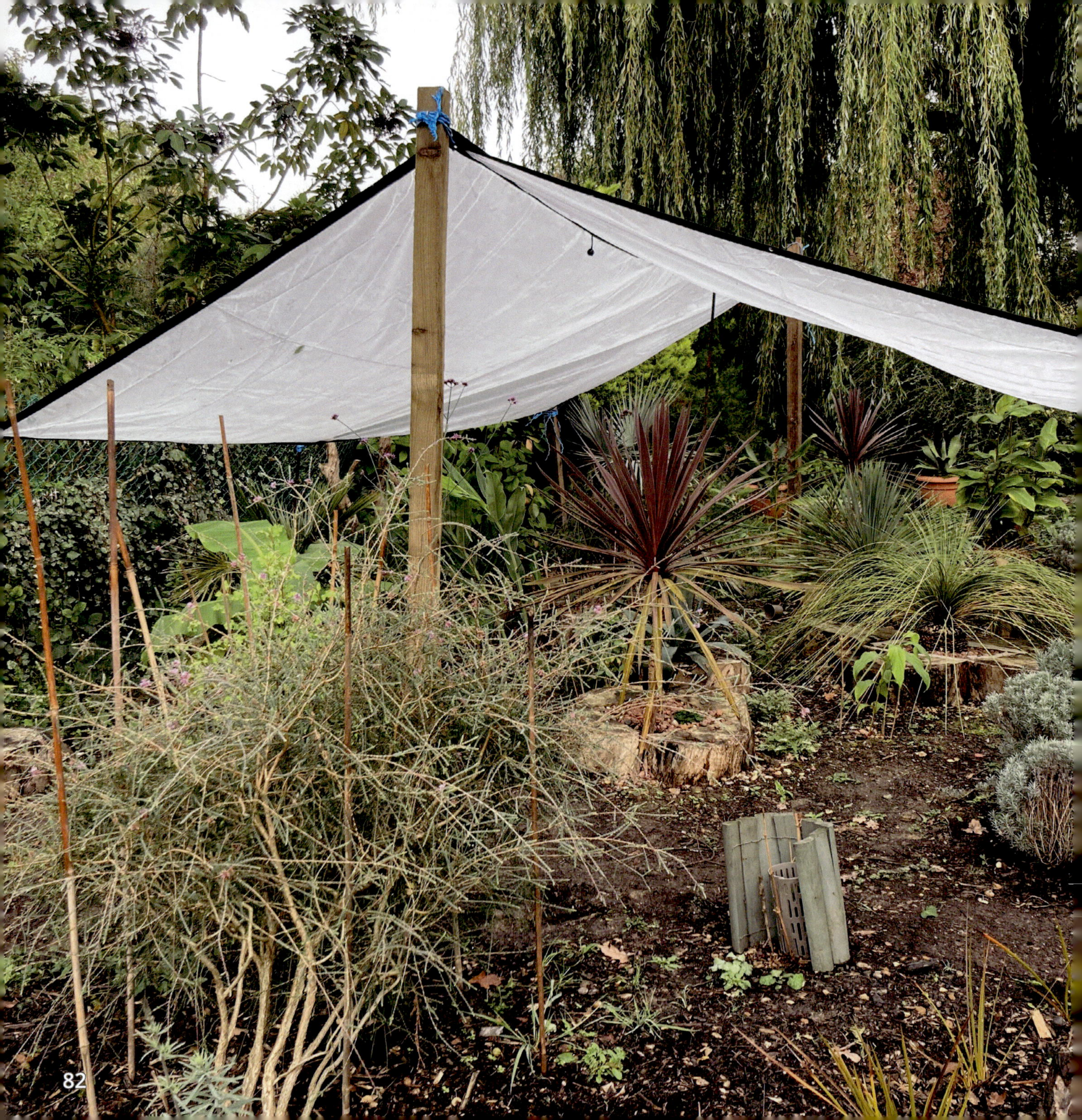

During the next few months we all took it in turns to bring in barrows full of this precious commodity. Lately we have started spreading it around after allowing it to compost down for a few months.

Necessary maintenance work also needed to be undertaken with the replacement of the old broken fence behind the new greenhouse.

As the year drew to a close, the exotic area was covered with tarpaulin in order to protect the plants from hard frost and winter wet. A couple of new containers made out of wire mesh have been created for composting material.

◀ The exotic area covered to protect it from the frost

▶ Wire mesh containers for composting

Half way through the process…

...to the finish line

▲ New batch of Corokia seedlings from Paul Boosey

# Conclusion

*T*WO YEARS HAVE PASSED since the beginning of this project. All the setbacks and challenges notwithstanding, I feel that the end result has far exceeded my expectations. I certainly didn't expect that the clearing, hard landscaping and most of the planting would have been completed within eighteen months.

The aim of reducing the new garden's carbon footprint to a minimum by recycling all available materials has also been achieved. Not only were logs and branches reused, but so were the left over concrete, bricks and builders' sand utilised as hardcore for the paths.

It's a far cry from the development of my previous garden, which required more than 300 tons of imported material in order to improve the quality of the soil — and to give the plants I wanted to cultivate the conditions they require in order to thrive, including raised beds and borders supported by granite sets.

▲ My own Corokia seedlings transplanted from my existing garden

I didn't rely on drawings or 3D computer simulation in order to come up with the design for the new space, but simply used the logs and shifted them around, following the natural contours and slope of the terrain.

The whole site has been divided into three main sections: The Exotic part; the Prairie, framed by a row of Mediterranean shrubs and trees behind it; and the Woodland area, all separated by an outer and an inner path converging on the new greenhouse.

Now that the garden has entered a time of hibernation, I look forward to observing and helping it settle into its new shape whilst the plants — including Corokia seedlings newly introduced from my existing garden — establish themselves and colonise their new home.

# Appendix: the plants

## Newly acquired plants

*Acer griseum*
*Eucalyptus nicholii*
*Melaleuca gibbosa*
Banana *Musa*
*Canna*
Purple *Cordyline*
*Brahea armata*
*Yucca rostrata*
*Pseudopanax* 'Bronze Eagle'
*Chamaerops cerifera*
*Cordyline* 'Atropurpurea'
*Dicksonia antarctica*
*Dicksonia fibrosa*
*Albizia julibrissin* 'Summer Chocolate'
*Lagerstroemia* 'White'
*Lagerstroemia* 'Burgundy Cotton'

*Tetrapanax Rex*
*Schefflera taiwaniana*
*Schefflera delavyi*
*Ficus*
*Ficus afghanistanica* 'Silver Lyre'
Large Olive tree
*Lophomyrtus*
*Olearia capillaris*
*Olearia traversii*
*Olearia paniculata*
*Olearia arborescens*
*Feijoa sellowiana aka Acca sellowiana*
Lavender – *Lavandula Munstead*
*Pistacia lentiscus*
Cypresses – *Cupressus sempervirens*

## Plants transferred from existing garden to Prairie

*Verbena bonariensis*
*Thalictrum flavour subspecies*
*Glaucum*
*Phlomis italica*

*Lithrum*
*Bidens*
*Persicaria polymorpha*
*Sanguisorba*

*Teasel Dispacus*
*Veronicastrum*
*Panicum Heavy Metal*

*Miscanthus* – various
*Cortaderia* – various
Ferns – various

## Other plants transferred from existing garden

*Arum italica*
*Aralia cordata*
*Fuchsia* – various
*Eleagnus Quicksilver*
*Rodgersia* – various
*Anemone japonica*
Unnamed *Corokia* – various
*Libertia peregrinans*
*Corokia x virgata* 'County Park Orange'

*Corokia buddleiodes*
*Corokia x virgata* 'Emerald and Jade'
*Euonymus alata*
*Lysimachia ciliata* 'Firecracker'
*Lysimachia ciliata*
*Restios*
*Muehlenbeckia*
*Uncinia*
*Libertia peregrinans*

## Some of the plants gifted by Garden Club London

Large fennels – *Foeniculum*
*Corokia x virgata* 'Yellow Wonder'
*Myrtus communis*
Cardoons – *Cynara cardunculus*
*Phlomis italica*
*Salvias* – shrubby, various

*Ballota*
*Marrubium supinum*
*Salvia sclarea*
*Agaves* – various
*Verbena*

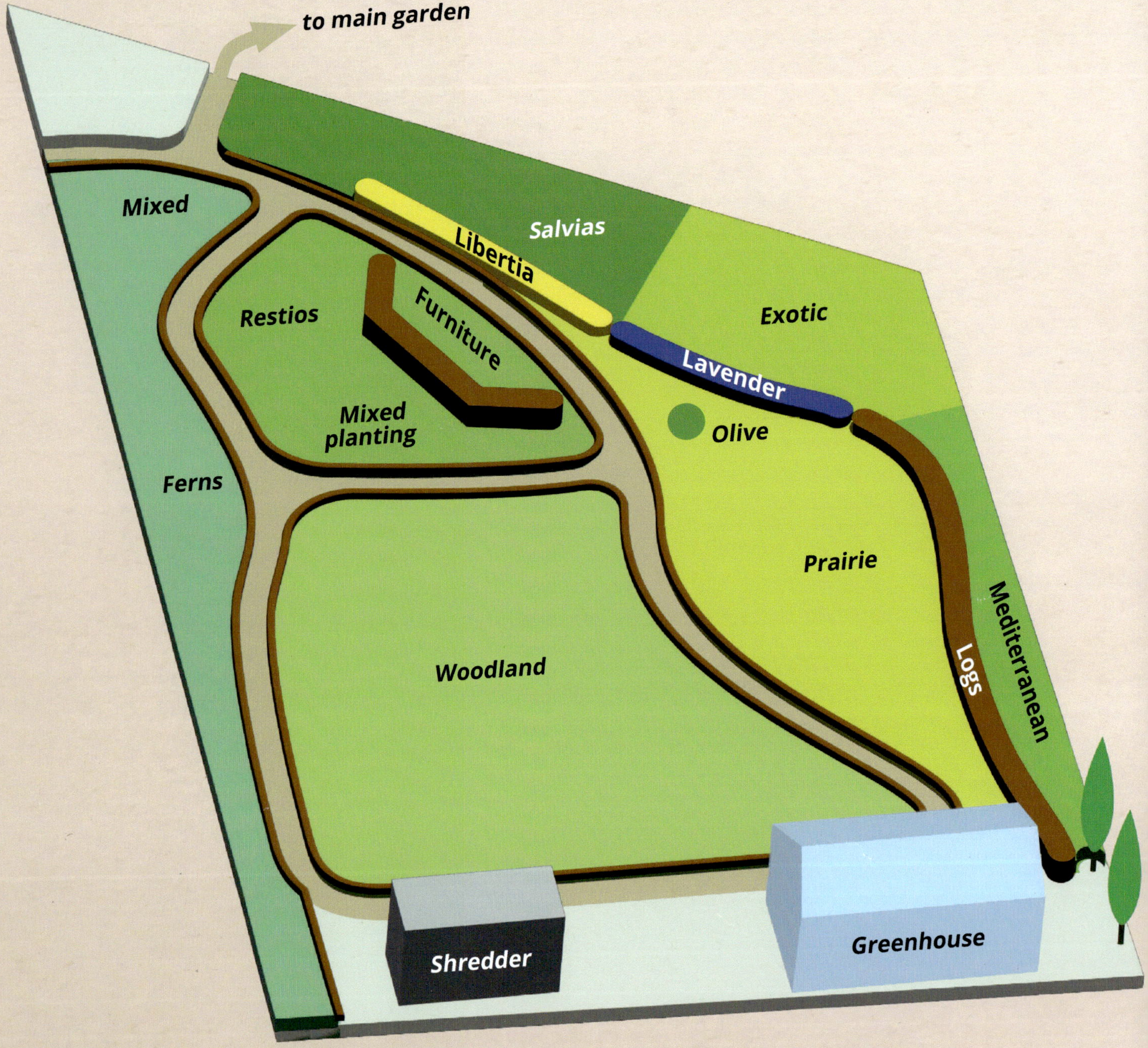
to main garden
Mixed
Salvias
Libertia
Restios
Furniture
Exotic
Lavender
Mixed planting
Olive
Ferns
Prairie
Mediterranean
Woodland
Logs
Shredder
Greenhouse